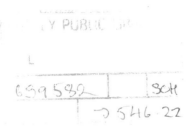

Series consultant: Dr Terry Jennings

Designed by Jane Tassie

The author and publishers would like to thank Siddika, Daniel
and the staff and pupils of the Charles Dickens J & I School, London,
for their help in making this book.

A CIP record for this book is available from the British Library.

ISBN 0-7136-6329-4

First paperback edition published 2002
First published 1999 by A & C Black Publishers Limited
37 Soho Square, London W1D 3QZ
www.acblack.com

Typeset in 23/28pt Gill Sans Infant and 25/27 pt Soupbone Regular

Printed in Singapore by Tien Wah Press (Pte.) Ltd

A & C Black uses paper produced with elemental chlorine-free pulp,
harvested from managed sustainable forests.

Science Explorers

Water

Exploring the science
of everyday materials

Nicola Edwards and
Jane Harris

Photographs by
Julian Cornish-Trestrail

A & C Black · London

Water is all around us!

Most of the water we use comes from rivers.

Rain makes rivers flow.

I'm watering this plant.
If I don't, it will die.

Water has to be cleaned before it is safe to drink.

I got this water from the tap.

It doesn't really taste or smell of anything, but it's nice and cold.

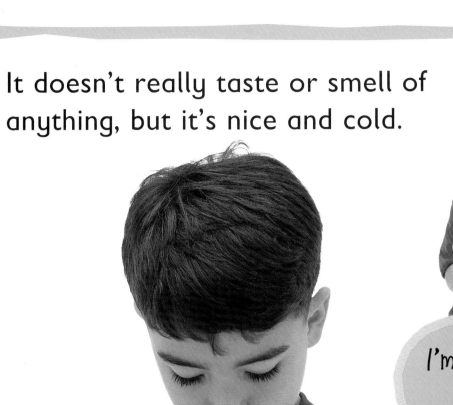

I'm not thirsty any more!

I can see the water moving up through my straw.

5

This tank is full of water.

I can see you on the other side.

I'm moving my hands about in the water.

The water's running down my arms.

It tickles!

7

We've collected all these things to see if they will float in the water.

This box is made of wood. It's heavy, so I wonder if it will sink.

It floats!

9

Oops! Some water
has splashed on
to my T-shirt and
made it wet.
It feels cold and
uncomfortable.

My plastic apron
is waterproof.
The water sits
on top of
the plastic
and doesn't
soak in.

What will happen
when I put
sugar in water
and stir it?

The sugar has disappeared.

But the water tastes really sweet. Ugh!

We're boiling water in a kettle.
Some of the water turns into steam.

Don't put your fingers near it.

This cold spoon was held in the steam. Look at the beads of water on the spoon.

The steam has turned back into water.

I'm pouring orange squash into a lolly mould.

And I've filled this balloon with water.

Now let's leave them in the freezer for a while.

I've taken the balloon out of the freezer.

Inside the balloon, there's a huge ball of ice. Wow!

It feels hard and cold.

My ice lolly
is ready, too.
It sticks to
my tongue.

Yummy!

The ball of ice has been left in the warm.

The ice is turning back into water.

19

I'm going to mix flour and water.

And I'm going to shake this jar of soil and water.

The flour and water make a sticky paste.

The soil doesn't mix very well. It settles in layers in the water.

These clothes are dirty. We're going to wash them with water and detergent.

Is it easier to wash clothes in warm water than in cold water?

My water's warmer than yours. My T-shirt is clean already.

Notes for parents and teachers

The aim of the *Science Explorers* series is to introduce children to ways of observing and classifying materials, so that they can discover the various properties which make them suitable for a range of uses. By talking about what they already know about materials from their everyday use of different objects, the children will gain confidence in making predictions about how a material will behave in different circumstances. Through their explorations, the children will be able to try out their ideas in a fair test.

pp 2–3

Water covers 71% of the earth's surface. The same amount of water exists on the planet today as during the time of the dinosaurs. Water is continually being recycled. It evaporates from the earth's surface to form clouds, then cools and condenses into rain and snow, and falls again to earth to collect in rivers, lakes and oceans. The oceans hold 97% of the earth's water and a further 2% is frozen in glaciers and ice caps. Fresh water forms less than 1% of the total supply.

Can the children describe what it is like to be outside when it is raining? How does the rain feel and sound? Discuss where they have encountered water in the natural environment and in the built environment.

Talk about the vital role of water in the lives of all living things. If possible, visit a pond with the children to see how water provides a habitat for a huge variety of plants and animals. The children could try growing two plants, watering one plant and not the other.

p 4

Water has to be treated before it is safe to drink. It is pumped from its source to a treatment plant via a screen which holds back any debris. Chemicals are added at the treatment plant. These cling to dirt and germs, forming cotton wool-like clumps of material which can be removed. The water is then filtered and disinfected, and stored in tanks and reservoirs.

Discuss the children's experience of water; in what kind of ways do they use water during the day at school and at home? How much water do they drink each day? Remind them that water may be 'hidden' in foods, such as fruit and bread.

pp 5–7

Pure water has no colour, smell or taste. It often contains tiny bubbles of gas which reflect the colours surrounding the water. The children could explore the many ways in which water can be made to move, such as by splashing, dripping, pouring, pumping, squirting, sprinkling and making ripples. The children could talk about their experiences of floating in and moving through water in a swimming pool.

pp 8–9

Ask the children if they can think why some things float while others sink. Can they predict how a range of differently shaped objects made of different materials will behave?

pp 10–11

The children could investigate a range of materials to test which absorb and which repel water. Explain that some fabrics are coated with a layer of plastic to make them waterproof.

pp 12–13, 20–21

The children could try a variety of activities to observe how adding water to different substances changes them. These could include adding water to dilute a concentrated fruit drink, adding water to dried soup powder, and seeing how bubble bath foams and changes the colour of the water when poured under a running tap. If possible, only allow the children to use plastic receptacles. If the children handle glass, ensure that they are properly supervised.

pp 14–15

The process of water boiling and turning to steam, then cooling and condensing into water droplets is an example of a reversible change. The children should watch a boiling kettle from a safe distance and be warned not to approach it; the cold spoon should be held in the steam only by an adult.

pp 16–19

The process of water freezing into solid ice, then thawing and turning back into liquid water is another example of a reversible change. The children should wear gloves when touching ice. Ice floats in water because water is heavier as a liquid than as a solid.

pp 22–23

The children could compare how effectively stains are removed using water with and without soap added (check for allergies to detergents), and using water of different temperatures.

Find the page

Here are some of the words and ideas in this book.